To _____

From _____

SELECTIONS FROM

Wings of Silver

Copyright © 1996 by The C. R. Gibson Company

Published by Garborg's Heart 'n Home, Inc.
P. O. Box 20132, Bloomington, MN 55420

Illustration by Mick Thurber

All rights reserved. No part of this book may be reproduced in
any form without permission in writing from the publisher.

Scripture quotations marked NIV are taken from the HOLY BIBLE,
NEW INTERNATIONAL VERSION® NIV®. Copyright © 1973,
1978, 1984 by International Bible Society. All rights reserved.

SPCN 5-5044-0294-8

Our grand business in life is not to see what lies dimly at a distance, but to do what lies clearly at hand.

JANUARY 1

∎

Nothing will make us so charitable and tender to the faults of others as to thoroughly examine ourselves.

DECEMBER 31

∎

The secret of success is constancy to purpose.

JANUARY 2

∎

If you don't get everything you want, think of the things you don't get that you don't want.

DECEMBER 30

.

Do not worry about your life, what you will eat or drink; or about your body, what you will wear. Is not life more important than food, and the body more important than clothes?

MATTHEW 6:25 NIV

JANUARY 3

There will be more rejoicing
in heaven over one sinner who
repents than over ninety-nine
righteous persons who do not
need to repent.

LUKE 15:7 NIV

DECEMBER 29

■

The language of love is understood by all.

JANUARY 4

∎

*God did not remove the Red
Sea, and He will lead us
through our difficulties when
they cannot be removed.*

DECEMBER 28

.

Love knows no limit to its endurance, no end to its trust, no fading of its hope; it can outlast anything.

JANUARY 5

∎

Youth and age look upon life from the opposite ends of the telescope: to the one it is exceedingly long; to the other, exceedingly short.

DECEMBER 27

∎

I know not what the future holds, but I know Who holds the future.

JANUARY 6

■

Draw near to God, and He will draw near to you.

DECEMBER 26

∎

Love still stands when all else has fallen.

JANUARY 7

.

---

*Be still, and know
that I am God!*

PSALM 46:10 NRSV

DECEMBER 25

∎

We know that in all things
God works for the good of
those who love him.

ROMANS 8:28 NIV

JANUARY 8

.

*The peace within becomes
the harmony without.*

DECEMBER 24

■

Make haste slowly.

JANUARY 9

■

A child's definition of house and home: "When you are outside, it looks like a house; but when you are on the inside, it feels like a home."

DECEMBER 23

.

When a friend asks, there is no tomorrow.

■

*Act as if each day were given
you for Christmas, just as
eager, just as proud!*

DECEMBER 22

■

*The greatest happiness of life
is the conviction that we are
loved, loved for ourselves,
or rather loved in spite
of ourselves.*

JANUARY 11

∎

Be devoted to one another in brotherly love. Honor one another above yourselves.

ROMANS 12:10 NIV

DECEMBER 21

■

The habit of expressing appreciation is oil on troubled waters. It is the essence of graciousness, kindness, and fair dealing. Fortunately, it is a habit that can be formed by anyone who will take the trouble.

JANUARY 12

■

Sing your song and your whole heart will be in the singing.

DECEMBER 20

.

*[God] is able to do immeasurably
more than all we ask or imagine,
according to his power that is
at work within us.*

EPHESIANS 3:20 NIV

JANUARY 13

∎

A child of God should
be a visible beatitude of joy
and happiness and a living
doxology for gratitude
and adoration.

DECEMBER 19

∎

Everything great is not always good, but all good things are great.

JANUARY 14

∎

*T*he trial of your faith is more
precious than gold.

DECEMBER 18

∎

Not where I breathe, but where I love, I live.

∎

*Delight yourself in the Lord
and he will give you the
desires of your heart.*

PSALM 37:4 NIV

DECEMBER 17

Love is the root of all virtues.

JANUARY 16

∎

*Reach out the hand of faith
and touch the throttle
of prayer.*

DECEMBER 16

∎

Happiness is neither within us only, or without us; it is the union of ourselves with God.

∎

*M*an looks on the outward
appearance; but God looks
on the heart.

DECEMBER 15

■

With God all things are possible.

MATTHEW 19:26 NIV

JANUARY 18

∎

The brightest blaze of intelligence is of less value than the smallest spark of charity.

DECEMBER 14

∎

---

*If at first you do succeed,
try something harder.*

JANUARY 19

.

Judge nothing before the appointed time; wait till the Lord comes.

1 CORINTHIANS 4:5 NIV

DECEMBER 13

.

*Love is to the moral nature
what the sun is to the earth.*

JANUARY 20

∎

*Take one step toward God,
and He will take two steps
toward you.*

DECEMBER 12

∎

God is only a prayer away.

JANUARY 21

■

God has two dwellings:
one in heaven and the other
in a meek and thankful heart.

DECEMBER 11

∎

Good manners are the small coin of virtue.

JANUARY 22

■

The things which are seen are temporal, but the things which are not seen are eternal.

∎

Know that the testing of your faith produces endurance; and let endurance have its full effect, so that you may be mature and complete, lacking in nothing.

JAMES 1:3,4 NRSV

JANUARY 23

By grace you have been saved through faith, and this is not your own doing; it is the gift of God.

EPHESIANS 2:8 NRSV

DECEMBER 9

■

*L*ove, like warmth, should
beam forth on every side and
bend to every necessity of
our brothers.

JANUARY 24

∎

*Faith does not exclude work,
but only the merit of work.*

DECEMBER 8

∎

The test of our love to God is the love we have one for another.

JANUARY 25

∎

*M*an should eat and drink
and enjoy the good of all his
labor; it is the gift of God.

DECEMBER 7

■

The goodness of God endures
continually.

JANUARY 26

.

*Sometimes faith must learn
a deeper rest,
And trust God's silence when
He does not speak.*

DECEMBER 6

■

Discover what is true and practice what is good.

JANUARY 27

■

All loves should be stepping stones to the love of God.

DECEMBER 5

■

I will lie down and sleep,
for you alone, O Lord,
make me dwell in safety.

PSALM 4:8 NIV

JANUARY 28

Jesus said: "Come to me,
all you that are weary and
are carrying heavy burdens,
and I will give you rest."

MATTHEW 11:28 NRSV

DECEMBER 4

∎

---

*Faith is the eyesight
of the soul.*

JANUARY 29

.

*The well of Providence is
deep. It's the buckets we
bring to it that are small.*

DECEMBER 3

■

*The remedy for wrongs is
to forget them.*

JANUARY 30

■

He is greatest who is most useful to others.

DECEMBER 2

■

*The secret of success
is hard work.*

JANUARY 31

∎

Faith grows in the valley.

DECEMBER 1

■

For this very reason, make every effort to add to your faith goodness; and to goodness, knowledge; and to knowledge, self-control; and to self-control, perseverance; and to perseverance, godliness; and to godliness, brotherly kindness; and to brotherly kindness, love.

2 PETER 1:5-7 NIV

FEBRUARY 1

∎

*Love understands
and love waits.*

NOVEMBER 30

■

*Whoever in prayer can say
"Our Father" acknowledges,
and should feel, the
brotherhood of the whole
race of mankind.*

FEBRUARY 2

Unless the Lord builds the house, those who build it labor in vain. Unless the Lord guards the city, the guard keeps watch in vain.

PSALM 127:1 NRSV

NOVEMBER 29

∎

You should love your neighbor as yourself, and you should be good to yourself.

FEBRUARY 3

■

*If we love one another,
God dwells in us.*

NOVEMBER 28

.

I am the bread of life. He who comes to me will never go hungry, and he who believes in me will never be thirsty.

JOHN 6:35 NIV

FEBRUARY 4

O for a thanksgiving for every heartbeat and a song for every breath.

NOVEMBER 27

■

*The secret of contentment
is knowing how to enjoy
what you have.*

FEBRUARY 5

■

*Never put a question mark
where God puts a period.*

NOVEMBER 26

.

Poise is the art of raising the eyebrows instead of the roof.

FEBRUARY 6

■

The blind with their hand in God's can see more clearly than those who can see and have no faith.

NOVEMBER 25

∎

We live by faith, not by sight.

2 CORINTHIANS 5:7 NIV

FEBRUARY 7

■

Teach me, Father, when I pray,
  Not to ask for more,
But rather let me give my thanks
  For what is at my door.
For food and drink, for gentle rain,
  For sunny skies above,
For home and friends, for peace and joy,
  But most of all for love.

NOVEMBER 24

▪

What we need is not new light, but new sight; not new paths, but new strength to walk in the old ones; not new duties but new strength from on high to fulfill those that are plain before us.

FEBRUARY 8

■

Whatever is true, whatever is noble, whatever is right, whatever is pure, whatever is lovely, whatever is admirable—if anything is excellent or praiseworthy—think about such things.

PHILIPPIANS 4:8 NIV

NOVEMBER 23

True prayer always receives what is asked or something better.

FEBRUARY 9

■

*P*ractice an attitude
of gratitude.

NOVEMBER 22

∎

Set your minds on things above, not on earthly things.

COLOSSIANS 3:2 NIV

FEBRUARY 10

Love ever gives and forgives.

NOVEMBER 21

∎

How empty learning,
How vain is art,
*But as it mends the life
And guides the heart.*

FEBRUARY 11

∎

When you have thanked the Lord for every blessing sent, little time will then remain for murmur or lament.

NOVEMBER 20

■

*Confront improper conduct,
not by retaliation, but
by example.*

FEBRUARY 12

∎

*Whoever believes in the Son
has eternal life.*

JOHN 3:36 NRSV

NOVEMBER 19

∎

If you have faith as small as a mustard seed, you can say to this mountain, "Move from here to there" and it will move. Nothing will be impossible for you.

MATTHEW 17:20 NIV

FEBRUARY 13

*Nothing can be truly great
which is not right.*

NOVEMBER 18

•

To love and be loved is the greatest happiness of existence.

FEBRUARY 14

■

The best remedy for discontent is to count our blessings.

NOVEMBER 17

∎

*Happiness or unhappiness
depends more on the way we
meet events than on the nature
of those events themselves.*

FEBRUARY 15

∎

*Continue in prayer and watch
in the same with thanksgiving.*

NOVEMBER 16

∎

---

*A true friend is forever
a friend.*

FEBRUARY 16

∎

From the errors of others a wise man corrects his own.

NOVEMBER 15

∎

May the words of my mouth and the meditation of my heart be pleasing in your sight, O Lord.

PSALM 19:14 NIV

FEBRUARY 17

∎

Love is patient. Love is kind.... It bears all things, believes all things, hopes all things, endures all things. Love never ends.

1 CORINTHIANS 13:4-8 NRSV

NOVEMBER 14

■

Good listeners are not only popular everywhere, but after a while they know something.

FEBRUARY 18

■

He who is not liberal with
what he has deceives himself
when he thinks he would be
liberal if he had more.

NOVEMBER 13

∎

*Recreation is not being idle;
it is easing the wearied part
by change of occupation.*

FEBRUARY 19

■

*M*oney dishonestly acquired is never worth its cost, while a good conscience never costs as much as it is worth.

NOVEMBER 12

■

I can do everything through him who gives me strength.

PHILIPPIANS 4:13 NIV

FEBRUARY 20

■

Some men have many reasons why they cannot do what they want, when all they need is one reason why they can.

NOVEMBER 11

■

*Be careful how you live;
you may be the only Bible
some people read.*

FEBRUARY 21

∎

As threshing separates the wheat from the chaff, so does affliction purify virtue.

NOVEMBER 10

■

We cannot give like God, but surely we may forgive like Him.

FEBRUARY 22

■

*God is not a God of disorder
but of peace.*

1 CORINTHIANS 14:33 NIV

NOVEMBER 9

■

Here, believe.
There, understand.

FEBRUARY 23

■

*I*t is better to suffer for
speaking the truth than that
the truth should suffer for
want of speaking it.

NOVEMBER 8

∎

God is love. Whoever lives in love lives in God, and God in him.

1 JOHN 4:16 NIV

FEBRUARY 24

The outlook may be dark, but the uplook is glorious.

NOVEMBER 7

∎

Enjoy present pleasures in such a way as not to injure future ones.

FEBRUARY 25

■

*Prove all things; hold fast
that which is good.*

NOVEMBER 6

■

The place to be happy is here.
The time to be happy is now.
The way to be happy is
to help make others happy.

FEBRUARY 26

■

*We reform others
unconsciously when
we walk uprightly.*

NOVEMBER 5

∎

*Our strength lies in our
dependence upon God.*

FEBRUARY 27

■

*Do good with what you
have, or it will do you
no good.*

NOVEMBER 4

.

Faith is being sure of what we hope for and certain of what we do not see.

HEBREWS 11:1 NIV

FEBRUARY 28

■

*Being rooted and grounded in love....
That you may have the power to
comprehend, with all the saints, what is
the breadth and length and height and
depth, and to know the love of Christ that
surpasses knowledge, so that you may be
filled with all the fullness of God.*

EPHESIANS 3:17-19 NRSV

NOVEMBER 3

∎

He gives the very best to those who leave the choice with Him.

FEBRUARY 29

■

There may be times when you cannot find help, but there is no time when you cannot give help.

NOVEMBER 2

∎

Happiness is a running stream.

MARCH 1

.

Toil awhile, endure awhile, believe always, and never turn back.

NOVEMBER 1

■

*The Lord is my shepherd,
I shall not be in want. He
makes me lie down in green
pastures, he leads me
beside quiet waters.*

PSALM 23:1,2 NIV

MARCH 2

∎

*Those that do good for good's
sake seek neither praise nor
reward, but they are sure
of both in the end.*

OCTOBER 31

■

If our love were but more simple,
We should take Him at His word,
And our lives would be all sunshine
In the sweetness of the Lord.

MARCH 3

.

*For kindness is indeed sublime
and worth the trouble anytime.
Sincerity is all we need
to help us do a friendly deed.*

OCTOBER 30

■

*We always have time enough,
if we but use it right.*

MARCH 4

.

*Who shall separate us
from the love of Christ?
Shall trouble or hardship
or persecution or famine or
nakedness or danger or sword?*

ROMANS 8:35 NIV

OCTOBER 29

▪

$\mathcal{I}$am the way, the truth, and the life. No one comes to the Father except through me.

JOHN 14:6 NIV

MARCH 5

■

The study of God's word for the purpose of discovering God's will is the secret discipline which has formed the greatest characters.

OCTOBER 28

.

The naked truth is not indecent.

MARCH 6

.

No man has a right to do as he pleases, except when he pleases to do right.

OCTOBER 27

·

Let those who put their trust in God rejoice: let them ever shout for joy because God defends them.

MARCH 7

*God listens to our hearts
rather than to our words.*

OCTOBER 26

∎

Trust in the Lord with all your heart and lean not on your own understanding; in all your ways acknowledge him, and he will make your paths straight.

PROVERBS 3:5,6 NIV

MARCH 8

∎

*Good depends not on things
but on the use we make
of things.*

OCTOBER 25

.

*The first step in making a
dream come true is to wake up.*

∎

*Be strong in faith,
giving glory to God.*

OCTOBER 24

■

*Those who trust in the Lord,
happy are they.*

MARCH 10

■

My brothers and sisters, whenever
you face trials of any kind, consider
it nothing but joy, because you know
that the testing of your faith
produces endurance.

JAMES 1:2,3 NRSV

OCTOBER 23

∎

*If I could only know the heartaches you have felt,
The longing for the things that never came,
I would not misconstrue your erring then,
Nor ever blame.*

MARCH 11

·

Better is a little with righteousness than great revenues without right.

OCTOBER 22

∎

God loves a cheerful giver.

2 CORINTHIANS 9:7 NIV

MARCH 12

∎

Happiness is enhanced by others but does not depend upon others.

OCTOBER 21

■

The purest pleasures are found in useful work.

MARCH 13

■

*If we ever have a golden age,
it will be because golden hearts
are beating in it.*

OCTOBER 20

■

To find fault is easy; to do better may be difficult.

MARCH 14

▪

*By this everyone will know
that you are my disciples, if you
have love for one another.*

JOHN 13:35 NRSV

OCTOBER 19

■

Nobody can be good to others without being good to themselves.

MARCH 15

■

A problem honestly stated
is half solved.

OCTOBER 18

■

This is the message you heard from the beginning: We should love one another.

1 JOHN 3:11 NIV

MARCH 16

■

Honesty is always the best policy.

OCTOBER 17

∎

We persuade others by being in earnest ourselves.

MARCH 17

■

Be what you say and say what you are.

OCTOBER 16

■

If your cup seems too bitter, if your burden seems too heavy, be sure that it is the wounded hand that is holding the cup, and that it is He who carries the cross that is carrying the burden.

MARCH 18

Nothing is pleasure that is not spiced with variety.

OCTOBER 15

■

All heaven is interested in the happiness of man.

MARCH 19

∎

Blessed are the meek, for they will inherit the earth.

MATTHEW 5:5 NIV

OCTOBER 14

Dear friends, since God so loved us, we also ought to love one another.

1 JOHN 4:11 NIV

MARCH 20

■

Should Thy mercy send me sorrow,
toil, and woe,
Or should pain attend me
on my path below;
Grant that I may never fail
Thy hand to see;
Grant that I may ever cast
my care on Thee.

OCTOBER 13

*Sow an act and you reap
a habit. Sow a habit and
you reap a character. Sow
a character and you reap
a destiny.*

MARCH 21

.

As you would that men should do to you, do you also to them likewise.

OCTOBER 12

.

No cloud can overshadow a
true Christian, but his faith
will discern a rainbow on it.

MARCH 22

■

A ship is safest in deep water.

OCTOBER 11

∎

Wisdom...is more precious than rubies; nothing you desire can compare with her. Long life is in her right hand; in her left hand are riches and honor.

PROVERBS 3:13,15,16 NIV

MARCH 23

∎

*He who masters his words
will master his works.*

OCTOBER 10

∎

The end of our faith is the salvation of our souls.

MARCH 24

.

Humble yourselves, therefore, under God's mighty hand, that he may lift you up in due time.

1 PETER 5:6 NIV

OCTOBER 9

∎

*There are no riches above a
sound body, and no joy above
the joy of the heart.*

MARCH 25

∎

*B*e not weary in well doing;
for in due season you shall
reap, if you faint not.

■

Remember there are no bad days—some are just better than others.

MARCH 26

■

*We must love all people
because God loves them
and wills to redeem them.*

OCTOBER 7

Those who sow in tears will reap with songs of joy.

PSALM 126:5 NIV

MARCH 27

*Can my creed be recognized
in my deed?*

OCTOBER 6

It is good to let a little
sunshine out as well as in.

MARCH 28

▪

*J*udge not, and you shall not
be judged: condemn not, and
you shall not be condemned:
forgive, and you shall
be forgiven.

OCTOBER 5

∎

The best way to succeed in life is to act on the advice you give to others.

MARCH 29

∎

*A cheerful heart is good
medicine, but a crushed
spirit dries up the bones.*

PROVERBS 17:22 NIV

OCTOBER 4

■

We can do anything we want to if we stick to it long enough.

MARCH 30

■

*Our deeds determine us
as much as we determine
our deeds.*

OCTOBER 3

■

Satisfy us in the morning with your unfailing love, that we may sing for joy and be glad all our days.

PSALM 90:14 NIV

MARCH 31

*To be without some of
the things you want is
an indispensable part
of happiness.*

■

He who can suppress a moment's anger may prevent a day of sorrow.

APRIL 1

■

*Be great in act, as you have
been in thought. Suit the action
to the word and the word to
the action.*

OCTOBER 1

■

*Your joy no one takes
from you.*

APRIL 2

▪

Blessed is the man who finds wisdom, the man who gains understanding, for she is more profitable than silver and yields better returns than gold.

PROVERBS 3:13,14 NIV

SEPTEMBER 30

∎

God will not look you over for medals, degrees, or diplomas, but for scars.

APRIL 3

■

*H*e that abides in Me, and
I in him, the same brings forth
much fruit: for without Me
you can do nothing.

SEPTEMBER 29

*God so loved the world that
he gave his one and only
Son, that whoever believes
in him shall not perish but
have eternal life.*

JOHN 3:16 NIV

APRIL 4

∎

*A real friend is one who
helps us to think our noblest
thoughts, put forth our best
efforts, and to be our
best selves.*

SEPTEMBER 28

■

Joy is everywhere. I am not fully dressed until I adorn myself with a smile of joy.

APRIL 5

■

A little more tired at the close of the day,
A little less anxious to have our way,
A little less anxious to scold and blame,
A little more care for a brother's name;
And so we are nearing the journey's end,
Where time and eternity meet and blend.

SEPTEMBER 27

A little more determination,
A little more pluck,
A little more work—
that's luck.

∎

*The fruit derived from labor
is the sweetest of pleasures.*

■

*He restores my soul.
He guides me in paths of
righteousness
for his name's sake.*

PSALM 23:3 NIV

APRIL 7

∎

The wisdom that comes from heaven is first of all pure; then peace-loving, considerate, submissive, full of mercy and good fruit, impartial and sincere.

JAMES 3:17 NIV

SEPTEMBER 25

∎

The supreme pleasure is to promote the joy of others.

APRIL 8

∎

Use your gifts faithfully, and they shall be enlarged; practice what you know, and you shall attain to higher knowledge.

∎

If you have knowledge, let others light their candles by it.

APRIL 9

∎

---

*That which is painful to the
body may be profitable
to the soul.*

SEPTEMBER 23

■

Pleasant words are a honeycomb, sweet to the soul and healing to the bones.

PROVERBS 16:24 NIV

APRIL 10

■

Love is the commandment for fulfilling all commandments— the rule for fulfilling all rules.

SEPTEMBER 22

■

Salvation is free, but being Christian is costly.

APRIL 11

■

A good name is more desirable than great riches; to be esteemed is better than silver or gold.

PROVERBS 22:1 NIV

SEPTEMBER 21

∎

Don't spend your days stringing and tuning your instrument—start making music now.

APRIL 12

∎

---

*To be happy at home is the
ultimate aim of all ambition.*

SEPTEMBER 20

∎

*H*appy are the people whose
God is the Lord.

PSALM 144:15 NRSV

APRIL 13

▪

Let me grow lovely, growing old—
so many fine things do:
Lace and ivory and gold
and silks need not be new.
There is healing in old trees,
old streets a glamour hold.
Why may not I, as well as these,
grow lovely, growing old?

SEPTEMBER 19

∎

Listening well is as important as talking well and is as essential to all conversation.

APRIL 14

.

Therefore, as we have opportunity, let us do good to all people, especially to those who belong to the family of believers.

GALATIANS 6:10 NIV

SEPTEMBER 18

■

The cloud that darkens the present hour may brighten all our future days.

APRIL 15

∎

Be not forgetful to entertain strangers: for thereby some have entertained angels unawares.

SEPTEMBER 17

■

Faith does not spring out of feeling, but feeling out of faith. The less we feel, the more we should trust.

APRIL 16

■

Sometimes a noble failure serves the world as faithfully as a distinguished success.

SEPTEMBER 16

∎

*Husbands, love your wives,
just as Christ loved the church
and gave himself up for her.*

EPHESIANS 5:25 NIV

APRIL 17

*Those who reform themselves
have done much toward
reforming others.*

SEPTEMBER 15

∎

Do not put off until
tomorrow what can
be enjoyed today.

APRIL 18

∎

Those who wait for the Lord shall renew their strength, they shall mount up with wings like eagles, they shall run and not be weary, they shall walk and not faint.

ISAIAH 40:31 NRSV

SEPTEMBER 14

■

Fear nothing so much as sin.

APRIL 19

■

Experience is what makes you wonder how it got a reputation for being the best teacher.

.

Contend for the faith that was once for all entrusted to the saints.

JUDE 1:3 NIV

APRIL 20

Happiness consists not in possessing much, but in being content with what we now possess.

SEPTEMBER 12

■

*Meekness is surrendering
to God.*

APRIL 21

■

This is love: not that we loved God, but that he loved us and sent his Son as an atoning sacrifice for our sins.

1 JOHN 4:10 NIV

SEPTEMBER 11

.

The spirit of melancholy would often take its flight from us if only we would take up the song of praise.

APRIL 22

∎

*Today's profits are yesterday's
goodwill ripened.*

SEPTEMBER 10

■

Since we have been justified through faith, we have peace with God through our Lord Jesus Christ.

ROMANS 5:1 NIV

APRIL 23

I have wept in the night
for the shortness of sight
That to somebody's need
made me blind;
But I never have yet
felt a twinge of regret
For being a little too kind.

SEPTEMBER 9

∎

*The prayer of the humble
pierces the clouds.*

APRIL 24

∎

When you pray, go into your room, close the door and pray to your Father, who is unseen. Then your Father, who sees what is done in secret, will reward you.

MATTHEW 6:6 NIV

SEPTEMBER 8

■

The rung of a ladder was never meant to rest upon, but only to hold a man's foot long enough to enable him to put the other one higher.

APRIL 25

■

Love, and you shall be loved.

SEPTEMBER 7

∎

Even though I walk through the valley of the shadow of death, I will fear no evil, for you are with me; your rod and your staff, they comfort me.

PSALM 23:4 NIV

APRIL 26

∎

Speak gently—
it is better far to rule by love than fear.
Speak gently—
let no harsh words mar the good we
might do here.

SEPTEMBER 6

∎

There are times when nothing we can say is nearly so powerful as saying nothing.

APRIL 27

∎

A glad heart makes a cheerful countenance.

PROVERBS 15:13 NRSV

SEPTEMBER 5

■

Believe in God, and He will help you; order your way aright, and trust in Him.

APRIL 28

∎

We cannot always oblige, but we can always speak obligingly.

SEPTEMBER 4

■

The prayer of a righteous man is powerful and effective.

JAMES 5:16 NIV

APRIL 29

∎

The real victory of faith is to trust God in the dark.

SEPTEMBER 3

∎

True greatness consists in being great in little things.

APRIL 30

■

All of you must clothe yourselves with humility in your dealings with one another, for "God opposes the proud, but gives grace to the humble."

1 PETER 5:5 NRSV

SEPTEMBER 2

This is maturity:
To be able to stick with a job until it is finished; to be able to bear an injustice without wanting to get even; to be able to carry money without spending it; and to do one's duty without being supervised.

MAY 1

■

The heart has reasons that reason does not understand.

.

Our light and momentary troubles are achieving for us an eternal glory that far outweighs them all.

2 CORINTHIANS 4:17 NIV

MAY 2

The virtue lies in the struggle, not in the prize.

AUGUST 31

.

To love is to place our happiness in the happiness of another.

MAY 3

.

*Rejoice in the Lord always.
I will say it again: Rejoice!*

PHILIPPIANS 4:4 NIV

AUGUST 30

∎

*Faith is the victory that
overcomes the world.*

MAY 4

∎

Love sees what no eye sees;
love hears what no ear hears.

AUGUST 29

■

*R*ejoice in the Lord and be glad, you righteous; sing, all you who are upright in heart!

PSALM 32:11 NIV

MAY 5

■

Discretion in speech is more than eloquence.

AUGUST 28

∎

One who is afraid of lying is usually afraid of nothing else.

MAY 6

∎

I am not ashamed of the gospel, because it is the power of God for the salvation of everyone who believes.

ROMANS 1:16 NIV

AUGUST 27

*Rest not from duty,
but find rest in it.*

MAY 7

.

Let those who suffer according to the will of God commit the keeping of their souls to Him in well doing, as unto a faithful Creator.

AUGUST 26

If God is for us, who can be against us?

ROMANS 8:31 NIV

MAY 8

.

He prays best who loves best.

AUGUST 25

■

*B*e persuaded that, what
He has promised, He is
able to perform.

MAY 9

■

Firmness is that admirable quality in ourselves that is merely stubbornness in others.

AUGUST 24

.

When you have accomplished your daily task, go to sleep in peace; God is awake!

■

Those who want to save their life will lose it, and those who lose their life for my sake will find it.

AUGUST 23

▪

Love is love's reward.

MAY 11

■

God knows us better than we know ourselves, and He loves us better too.

AUGUST 22

.

I have learned to be content whatever the circumstances.

PHILIPPIANS 4:11 NIV

MAY 12

∎

The late blooming virtues can be the very best.

AUGUST 21

■

A good memory is fine—but the ability to forget is the true test of greatness.

MAY 13

∎

Wait on the Lord; be of good courage, and He shall strengthen your heart. Wait, I say, on the Lord!

PSALM 27:14 NKJV

AUGUST 20

■

The evening of a well-spent life brings its lamp with it.

MAY 14

■

*An ounce of pluck is worth
a ton of luck.*

AUGUST 19

■

The Bible is a surer and safer guide through life than human reason.

MAY 15

∎

The greatest truths are the simplest; and so are the greatest men.

AUGUST 18

.

Ask in faith, never doubting, for the one who doubts is like a wave of the sea, driven and tossed by the wind.

JAMES 1:6 NRSV

MAY 16

■

I consider that our present
sufferings are not worth
comparing with the glory
that will be revealed in us.

ROMANS 8:18 NIV

AUGUST 17

∎

If you were to list the ten smartest people, who would be the other nine?

MAY 17

■

Talent knows what to do; tact knows when and how to do it.

AUGUST 16

.

Whatever He sends, whether sunshine or dew, is needed for your soul's health.

MAY 18

■

*He is richest who is content
with the least.*

AUGUST 15

.

The grass is greener on the other side, but it is just as hard to mow.

MAY 19

.

It is only imperfection that is intolerant of what is imperfect. The more perfect we are, the more gentle and quiet we become toward the defects of others.

AUGUST 14

.

Think little of what others think of you.

MAY 20

■

We do not lose heart. Though outwardly we are wasting away, yet inwardly we are being renewed day by day.

2 CORINTHIANS 4:16 NIV

AUGUST 13

■

Do not be anxious about anything, but in everything, by prayer and petition, with thanksgiving, present your requests to God. And the peace of God, which transcends all understanding, will guard your hearts and your minds in Christ Jesus.

PHILIPPIANS 4:6,7 NIV

MAY 21

▪

*Silence is one of the great arts
of conversation.*

AUGUST 12

∎

Do the truth you know, and you shall learn the truth you need to know.

MAY 22

∎

It is by those who have suffered that the world is most advanced.

AUGUST 11

■

*Great victories come,
not through ease, but
by fighting valiantly and
meeting hardships bravely.*

MAY 23

. ∎

A righteous man may have many troubles, but the Lord delivers him from them all.

PSALM 34:19 NIV

AUGUST 10

∎

It is easier to fight for one's principles than to live up to them.

∎

*Make the most of the best
and the least of the worst.*

AUGUST 9

∎

If there is anything better than to be loved, it is loving.

MAY 25

∎

To accept good advice is but to increase one's own ability.

AUGUST 8

■

Teach us to number our days aright, that we may gain a heart of wisdom.

PSALM 90:12 NIV

MAY 26

∎

Surely goodness and mercy shall follow me all the days of my life, and I shall dwell in the house of the Lord my whole life long.

PSALM 23:6 NRSV

AUGUST 7

Prayer is the key in the hand of faith which unlocks heaven's storehouse.

MAY 27

▪

Fundamentally true ideas possess greater ultimate power than physical might.

AUGUST 6

■

We cannot be happy unless we think we are the means of good to others.

MAY 28

∎

Christianity has not been tried and found wanting; it has been found difficult and not tried.

AUGUST 5

.

*Godliness with contentment
is great gain.*

1 TIMOTHY 6:6 NIV

MAY 29

■

No temptation has seized you except what is common to man. And God is faithful; he will not let you be tempted beyond what you can bear. But when you are tempted, he will also provide a way out so that you can stand up under it.

1 CORINTHIANS 10:13 NIV

AUGUST 4

∎

*P*ure gold can lie for
a month in the furnace
without losing a grain.

MAY 30

∎

The joy of the Lord is your strength.

AUGUST 3

■

It is those who do their duties in everyday and trivial matters who fulfill them on great occasions.

MAY 31

■

*Life is a steep grade, and
we should welcome every
opportunity to give our friends
a lift when they need it.*

AUGUST 2

∎

Humility is the solid foundation of all the virtues.

JUNE 1

■

*The prayer of the upright
is His delight.*

PROVERBS 15:8 NKJV

AUGUST 1

■

The real purpose of our existence is not to make a living, but to make a life— a worthy, well-rounded, useful life.

JUNE 2

∎

You and I cannot determine what other men shall think and say about us. We can only determine what they ought to think of us and say about us.

∎

Blessed is the man who finds wisdom.... Her ways are pleasant ways, and all her paths are peace. She is a tree of life to those who embrace her.

PROVERBS 3:13,17,18 NIV

JUNE 3

■

Mastery in any art comes only with long practice.

JULY 30

∎

Never marry but for love; but see that you love what is lovely.

JUNE 4

∎

I have fought the good fight, I have finished the race, I have kept the faith. Now there is in store for me the crown of righteousness, which the Lord, the righteous Judge, will award to me on that day.

2 TIMOTHY 4:7,8 NIV

JULY 29

■

*Consider how the lilies grow.
They do not labor or spin. Yet I
tell you, not even Solomon in
all his splendor was dressed
like one of these.*

LUKE 12:27 NIV

JUNE 5

■

Patience is not passive; on the contrary, it is active; it is concentrated strength.

JULY 28

■

*Faith and meekness are
a delight to God.*

JUNE 6

■

Not everyone who says to me, "Lord, Lord," will enter the kingdom of heaven, but only he who does the will of my Father who is in heaven.

MATTHEW 7:21 NIV

JULY 27

■

How men treat us will make
little difference when we know
we have God's approval.

JUNE 7

∎

*I*n youth we run
into difficulties; in age
difficulties run into us.

JULY 26

∎

Trust in the Lord and do good; dwell in the land and enjoy safe pasture.

PSALM 37:3 NIV

JUNE 8

■

God sometimes washes the eyes of His children with tears, that they may read aright His providence and His commandments.

JULY 25

▪

When you begin to coast, you know you're on the downgrade.

JUNE 9

■

Parents who wish to train their children in the way they should go, must go in the way which they would have their children go.

JULY 24

.

To err is human;
to forgive is divine.

JUNE 10

∎

Be kind to one another, tenderhearted, forgiving one another, as God in Christ has forgiven you.

EPHESIANS 4:32 NRSV

JULY 23

∎

I will say of the Lord, "He is my refuge and my fortress, my God, in whom I trust."

PSALM 91:2 NIV

JUNE 11

The same furnace that liquefies the gold hardens the clay.

JULY 22

.

They also serve who only stand and wait.

JUNE 12

■

The dictionary is the only place success comes before work.

JULY 21

■

If you can't have the best of everything, make the best of everything you have.

JUNE 13

∎

If it is possible, as far as it depends on you, live at peace with everyone.

ROMANS 12:18 NIV

JULY 20

■

Whatever is worth doing at all, is worth doing well.

JUNE 14

■

*Faith takes God at His word,
whatever He says.*

JULY 19

▪

*Be strong and courageous....
Do not be afraid or discouraged,
for the Lord God, my God, is
with you. He will not fail you
or forsake you.*

1 CHRONICLES 28:20 NIV

JUNE 15

•

Those that love wisdom love life; and they that seek her early shall be filled with joy.

JULY 18

■

*Men do not fail;
they give up trying.*

JUNE 16

∎

Casting all your care upon Him, for He cares for you.

1 PETER 5:7 NKJV

JULY 17

The grinding that would wear away to nothing a lesser stone merely serves to give luster to a diamond.

JUNE 17

■

Faith is the awareness of utter helplessness without God.

JULY 16

∎

Rejoice with those who rejoice.

ROMANS 12:15 NIV

JUNE 18

■

You that fear the Lord, wait for His mercy; and go not aside, lest you fall.

JULY 15

■

Difficulties strengthen the mind, as labor does the body.

JUNE 19

■

*You prepare a table before
me in the presence of my
enemies. You anoint my head
with oil; my cup overflows.*

PSALM 23:5 NIV

JULY 14

∎

*The man who rows the boat
doesn't have time to rock it.*

JUNE 20

∎

Remember there's blue sky behind the blackest cloud.

JULY 13

.

*Do not be overcome by evil,
but overcome evil with good.*

ROMANS 12:21 NIV

JUNE 21

.

*Trouble and perplexity drive
me to prayer, and prayer drives
away perplexity and trouble.*

JULY 12

■

Anytime a man takes a stand, there'll come a time when he'll be tested to see how firmly his feet are planted.

JUNE 22

.

All people are born equal.
Each has a right to earn his
niche by the sweat of his brow.
But some sweat more and
carve larger niches.

JULY 11

■

A wife doubles a man's pleasures and divides his cares.

JUNE 23

First take the plank out of your own eye, and then you will see clearly to remove the speck from your brother's eye.

MATTHEW 7:5 NIV

JULY 10

∎

Free enterprise gives everybody a chance to get to the top. Some depend too much on the free and not enough on the enterprise.

JUNE 24

■

Troubles are often the tools by which God fashions us for better things.

JULY 9

■

*The Lord is with me; I will
not be afraid. What can
man do to me?*

PSALM 118:6 NIV

JUNE 25

∎

If I could only see the road you came,
With all the jagged rocks
and crooked ways,
I might more kindly think
of your misstep,
And only praise.

JULY 8

■

The most generous vine, if not pruned, runs out into many superfluous stems and grows at last weak and fruitless; so does the best man if he be not cut short in his desires and pruned with afflictions.

JUNE 26

■

Any trouble that is too small to take to God in prayer is too small to worry about.

JULY 7

∎

*What you are thunders so
loudly I cannot hear
what you say.*

JUNE 27

.

*The quitter never wins.
The winner never quits.*

JULY 6

.

---

*A smooth sea never made
a skillful mariner.*

JUNE 28

.

Humble yourselves before the Lord, and he will lift you up.

JAMES 4:10 NIV

JULY 5

■

The Lord has done great things for us, and we are filled with joy.

PSALM 126:3 NIV

JUNE 29

▪

Don't lessen the lesson.

JULY 4

.

You can tell some people aren't afraid of work by the way they fight it.

JUNE 30

■

The error of youth is to believe that intelligence is a substitute for experience, while the error of age is to believe that experience is a substitute for intelligence.

JULY 3

■

*Consider the blameless,
observe the upright; there is
a future for the man of peace.*

PSALM 37:37 NIV

JULY 1

*A cheerful friend is like
a sunny day.*

JULY 2

.